WHEN SOMETHING WONDERFUL ENDS

a history

a one woman, one barbie play

Sherry Kramer

I0141365

BROADWAY PLAY PUBLISHING INC
New York
www.broadwayplaypub.com
info@broadwayplaypub.com

WHEN SOMETHING WONDERFUL ENDS
© Copyright 2005, 2019 Sherry Kramer

Cover art by Karen Berry

First published by B P P I in December 2007
This edition, revised: July 2019
I S B N: 978-0-88145-839-8

Book design: Marie Donovan
Page make-up: Adobe InDesign
Typeface: Palatino

for my mother and father

WHEN SOMETHING WONDERFUL ENDS premiered at the Humana Festival of New American Plays at the Actors Theater of Louisville (Marc Masterson, Artistic Director) in March 2007. This was a co-production with InterAct Theater of Philadelphia (Seth Rozin, Artistic Director). The cast and creative contributors were:

WOMAN .... Lori Wilner

Director .... Tom Moore
Scenic designer .... Paul Owen
Costume designer .... Lorraine Venberg
Lighting designer .... Brian J Lilienthal
Video designer .... Jason Czaja
Properties designer .... Mark Walston
Stage manager .... Michele Traub
Dramaturg .... Carrie Hughes
Assistant dramaturg .... Diana Grisanti
Casting .... Andrew Zerman
Directing assistant .... Kyle J Schmidt

WHEN SOMETHING WONDERFUL ENDS was
subsequently produced by Red Then and Rude
Mechanicals in Austin with its first public performance
on 15 May 2008. The cast and creative contributors
were:

WOMAN...Barbara Chisholm
Director .... Katie Pearl
Scenic & costume designer .... Michal Raiford
Lighting designer ....Natalie George
Video & sound ....Lowell Bartholomee
Properties .... Holly Jackson
Stage manager ....Jennifer Anderson
Dramaturg .... Robert Faires
Technical director ....Thomas Graves

ACKNOWLEDGMENTS

WHEN SOMETHING WONDERFUL ENDS was developed at PlayLabs, Polly Carl, Artistic Director; The Bay Area Playwrights Festival, Amy Mueller, Artistic Director; and the Ojai Playwrights Conference, Bob Egan, Artisitic Director. The author wishes to thank Seth Rozin, Adrien-Alice Hansel, and Marc Masterson for their courage and faith; everyone at A T L for making working there a luminous experience; Linda Gehringer, Jeri Lynn Cohen, Melissa Kievman, and Jayne Wenger for their contributions to the play, their generosity, and their grace; Victor D'Altorio for his passionate work on the early drafts of this play; Barbara Chisholm, Katie Pearl, Michael Raiford and the Rude Mechs for making something wonderful in Austin; and Tom Moore for his wisdom, his vision, and the enduring gifts of a joyful collaboration.

CHARACTERS

ONE WOMAN, *a Midwestern Reform Jewish baby boomer.*
She has black curly hair.

ONE BARBIE, *a 1964 near mint Bubble Cut Brunette.*
The part was originally written for a mint condition, 1964
Redhead Swirl Ponytail Barbie, #850. The Swirl Ponytail
Barbie has an unusual ponytail, which is caught in back with
a yellow ribbon. Once taken down, as most little girls did
immediately, it was almost impossible to return to its former
swirly glory. I did not take my Barbie's ponytail down.
She is MC—mint condition. The role has recently been re-
written for a brunette bubblecut, near mint. However, in
general, any classic Barbie from the 1961-65 era will do.
Any hair color, and either style—ponytail or bubblecut.
Barbies in less than mint condition are of course also invited
to audition.

SET

The set might look like a room in a 50's split-level home, or it might be just a large square of bright red carpet, or it might be something in-between. There are probably lots of packing boxes around.

There are titles in the play. They might be presented in a way compatible with that of a 6th grade classroom presentation in 1964. Or some might be "broadcast" on an old console T V, and others might be written by the actress on boxes or any surface she can find. Or they might all be discovered in different, surprising and magical ways—the set might be like an advent calendar, with titles hiding, waiting to ambush and delight the audience. In the best sense, the titles can function like a treasure hunt for the audience. The timing of the titles in the text is not absolute, they may happen earlier or later than they do in the text, and productions may choose to do most, but not 100% of the titles...each production should make its own path through this element of the play.

There are Barbie clothes, and a tangerine and turquoise 1964 Barbie Dream Car with a dented front fender. There is a 1964 Brunette Barbie, still in her box, and a pile of vintage/ vintage approximate Barbie outfits. Four specific outfits— clothing and their accessories—are essential: Enchanted Evening; Red Flare; Nighty Negligee; and Senior Prom. (Three other outfits are not essential but helpful: Tennis, Anyone; Ski Queen; and Solo in the Spotlight.) A pile of unmatched Barbie shoes. A smaller pile of Ken clothes, and possibly another Barbie or two and a couple spare Kens. A vintage Barbie Dream House, either the original Dream House or Barbie's New Dream House, with at least most of their cardboard furnishings. And a lot of Ziplock bags. Throughout the play, as appropriate, the actress sorts Barbie clothes, and puts them in Ziplock bags.

CANDY

(The actress hands out Brach's cinnamon discs to audience members as they enter the theatre. Or perhaps the ushers do it. But it would be better if the actress does it. She, or the ushers, can invite the audience to unwrap the candies before, or after, but not during the show.)

TITLE:
WHEN SOMETHING WONDERFUL ENDS

When something wonderful ends, everybody wants
to know how it happened. "How did it come to this,"
they like to say. And "Why didn't we see it coming in
time." They like saying that, a lot. They get a kind of
common bewildered comfort from it. And then they
get tired of saying it. They get tired of the comfort that
not knowing brings.

Here's the good news. I *know* how it came to this. I
know why we didn't see it coming. I even know the
exact moment the end started and where I was at the
time.

I was at the Toy Box on the Plaza, Springfield,
Missouri's first shopping center, situated five miles
south of downtown, on historic Route 66. Now,
spending money at a shopping center five miles south
of downtown meant that the downtown, finding itself
the road not taken, would one day, soon, wither and
fade, so the Age of Enlightenment wasn't the only
thing dying at this moment, the downtown was too—
and not emblematically, but physically, it was really
and truly and specifically dying because I was buying
a dress. A dress with a name. A dress called Enchanted
Evening. Okay, my mother was buying it for me. I
was ten years old, so my mother put me in the car. In
the front seat, of the car. The world looked different
back then, the un-Ralph Nader changed world, no
car seats, not even any seat belts, you could run the
hell all over the car. When we took family trips in the
station wagon, mom and dad took a little mattress
and spread it out in the back and then it was nap time,

party time, the three of us kids, all the way to Cape
Cod three times and Miami Beach twice. Oh, and there
were cigarette ads everywhere before Nader changed
the world. Remember how great cigarette commercials
looked? Sexy women, manly men? My mother smoked
Herbert Tarytons, the most elegant pack of cigarettes
in the world. White background, and no design but
this lovely regal blue crown. I don't think the Tarytons
killed her. Of course, you can't be sure of much of
anything nowadays. So, anyway, my mother plopped
me into the car, and drove us from our house in
Brentwood, Springfield's very first subdivision, to the
Toy Box on the Plaza, where I was allowed to pick out,
from a whole wall of boxes filled with unimaginable
delight—one outfit.

(She brings out Enchanted Evening.)

This is Enchanted Evening. I think it cost a dollar fifty.
A Barbie only cost three seventy-five. I know because I
still have the box.

*(She brings out her Barbie, still in the box. She takes the
Barbie out of the box.)*

This is a Bubble Cut Brunette Barbie, a model made
between 1962 and 1964. She is a basic Barbie, nothing
really rare about her. Solid, unremarkable, excellent
condition but not exactly mint.

(She dresses Barbie in Enchanted Evening.)

Enchanted Evening is a classic Barbie outfit. A pink
satin evening gown with a huge, full, round train, the
skirt gathered up tight at the waist with a pink rose,
which causes it to start off as a tight sheath, then falls
in graceful folds that create an elegant drape. A great
look, especially if you don't actually have to walk
in it. It's from the Golden Age of Barbie, 1959-65. It
is one of the most valuable of all the Barbie outfits I
have—worth three thousand dollars, N R F P—Never

Removed From Package, or three hundred fifty dollars, M C—mint condition, with *all* the accessories. These include—

(She holds up each one as she mentions them.)

—a white fur stole lined with pink satin. Sparkly pink plastic shoes. Pearls. Pearl earrings. And opera length gloves. And you can forget about the big money if it's not mint—twenty bucks on eBay, if it's missing an earring or is worn or discolored in any way.

My Enchanted Evening is not worn. It is mint. It's almost as if I'd never played with it. None of my Barbie clothes—and I have fifty-nine outfits, virtually everything manufactured by Mattel from 1960 to 1965—none of these fifty-nine outfits—with the exception of a corduroy jumper with felt poodle appliqué called Friday Night Date which is stained and discolored and may actually belong to Sara Thomas, from across the street—none of my outfits show any sign of being worn at all. Enchanted Evening looks as good as the day I bought it. March 4, 1964.

And this is how I discovered that that very day was the start of the end of something wonderful.

I was driving back to Springfield to begin the long process of packing up my parents' home a few months ago, listening to a book on tape about the U.S. and the Middle East. It astonished me. I realized that while I had been acquiring Enchanted Evening, serial number 783, for my bubble cut Barbie, serial number 750, at the *exact same moment*, a SOFA, or Status Of Forces Agreement—S-O-F-A, had just been made the official law of the land. Not this land. Iran. Status of Forces Agreements are common, we sign then whenever our troops are stationed in foreign lands, but this SOFA started the cascade of events that lifts the Ayatollah Khomeini, until then a mild mannered cleric minding his own Islamic business, into a rabid dog of rage, launching his career as the official Islamist godfather of hate until he passes the baton to Osama, though not directly, we'll get to that, who then launches two planes into the Twin Towers, one into the Pentagon, and one into the ground. Which then launches America's attack on Iraq. Which then—well, we're just at *that* which then.

TITLE:
THE WHICH THEN

Here's what the which-then looks like, from my point of view, the place from which I am packing up the house and sorting my Barbie clothes and watching America's dream go bad.

I am on my way to the cemetery, to put some gladiolas on my mother's grave. It's a frail, magical ritual, a little bit like performing a miracle—doing something beautiful for the dead. It's impossible, of course, to do anything for the dead, but we still do it—my mother brought flowers to her mother's grave, and now I'm doing it for her. The willfulness of the miracle appeals to me. On the way to the cemetery, it's easy to believe in contact with the unseen, the divine, it's easy to believe that the small miracle you're about to perform will somehow be enough. On your way home from the cemetery it's different. This sudden ache hits you, because you've performed the miracle, and nothing changes. It is *not* enough. You pull out of the cemetery and that's it. Miracle over.

I have a Picture of the Miracle.

(*She shows a picture of gladiolas at her mother's grave. Then she shows four or five more pictures.*)

I don't remember when I started taking these pictures, but I have hundreds of them. It's some sort of documentary impulse, I suppose. I won't be coming back to Springfield after we sell the house, and these pictures will be the only way I'll be able to visit her grave. When I look at them I feel a little comfort. I know that photos don't have any real power, I know they aren't real miracles, they're just pictures of miracles. And I know that the miracles they are pictures of are small. Small miracles that don't have the power to transform the world beyond the cemetery gates.

Most of the other graves in the cemetery have artificial flowers on them. I think that the flowers I put on my mother's grave are *better* than the artificial ones people put on the graves of their loved ones, nearby. I think that the miracle *I* make is better then the miracle *they* make.

And I think this: that anytime a person puts *their* miraculous ritual with their dead above somebody *else's* miraculous ritual with theirs, means the start of something very unfine. In my case, the unfineness manifests itself as a little arrogant smug smallness. This smallness does two things. It files down some of the finer points of my soul, and this filing down process, it's cumulative, it's catastrophic, it will show up in twenty years as a dull, dead place at my very center. And the other thing it does is put me squarely in a vast historical context. My grieving heart has landed me smack dab in the center of a ritual that has had some of the ugliest unintended consequences the world has ever known. Miraculous rituals with the dead are the very heart of all religious belief—especially now that we don't spend a lot of time appeasing the weather and the crop gods.

One of the sadder things about life on this planet is
that half of all the rotten things people do to each
other start out as miracles they're trying to do for their
dead. Filling up the pyramid of someone you love with
lots of nice things to eat in the next life—thoughtful.
Burying seven thousand slaves alive to help them
around the house on the other side—not. I slipped a
piece of wrapped candy into my mother's hand, as we
left her. A Brach's cinnamon disc—her favorite candy,
my favorite candy. Giving her a token—a little sweet
to bribe the gods, or tip the boatman, seemed terribly
significant at the time. And not just significant—but
necessary. Because when your mother dies, and you
are, in some way that makes no sense at all and all
the sense in the world, dragged pretty far along with
her into that other place—you *understand* the *point*
of *religion*—to issue the passports and publish the
train schedules and arrange the passage that is the
transformation of the living into the dead. In the end,
all religion is basically just a construct to organize
what happens after. To hold back the night. The
reform Jewish night, by the way, is incredibly long and
completely dark, because Reform Jews don't believe in
heaven or hell.

The fear of death is the thing that drives all our drives.

Of course, the modern age has a new kind of drive.
This kind.

(She takes out Barbie's Dream Car.)

This is Barbie's Dream Car.

That's its actual name, the Dream Car. When you
put Barbie in it, you dreamed about the day you'd
be behind the wheel. But the thing about driving in
your dreams is—you never run out of gas. Because
running out of gas—as U.S. policy in the Middle East
for the past 50 years will attest to—is a nightmare.

A nightmare about oil—about oil and America, the Miracle Nation.

TITLE:
AMERICA, THE MIRACLE NATION

The miraculous thing about America is that we're an Enlightenment Nation. Many of our founding fathers were Deists, a religion that believed in God the watchmaker—God made the watch, and then let it run. So when they invented America, they insisted on the separation of church and state.

Most religions encourage you to prove your love for God by making other people love Him—kind of like forcing people to friend your best friend on Facebook. Some religions go further—they require you to torture and kill anyone who won't friend your Friend, and pile up their bodies to prove your commitment to the Friendship. Pile the bodies high enough, some religions say, and you can climb them like a ladder all the way to God. Deism didn't do any of these things. God rewarded us for nothing. Goodness was its own reward and there was no other. This made a blueprint for a new kind of country. America is the child of Deists like Tom Jefferson, who was the intellectual child of the most famous Deist of all, David Hume, whose writings directly inspired the Declaration and the Constitution. And David Hume's nickname, for anyone who is interested in these things, was The Great Infidel. Just so you know who your Daddy is.

Before America, there was no such thing as a nation where church and state were separate. In the old worlds, governments were a franchise arrangement, God was the *owner*—we were just the *operators*. Not in America. In America we're the owners, and it's always been a Mom and Pop store. God was just a shareholder at the very best, and he owned a *minimal* amount of stock. Sundays. He owned Sundays. And a few Catholic schools. He did not have the controlling shares in a country for the first time in history.

Once America existed, the world changed, from a vertical world to a horizontal one. "We the people" versus "the glory of God." The different use of your fellow human beings, in a horizontal world instead of a vertical one, is night and day.

The problem with fundamentalist countries is that they're still engaged in the old *vertical* relationship with God that gets played out *horizontally*—God's up there, they're down here, and they don't have any way to climb up there and be one with Him without building a ladder, and that ladder has always been, and seems like it will continue to be made out of the bodies of unbelievers.

Mostly, Americans live fully in the horizontal world. Yes, we climb over each other, but we don't do it for God. We do it for ourselves. We didn't wipe out our Infidels for religious reasons—the Indians were just in the way of our appetite, our huge, unstoppable greed, and after we wiped them out, the word Infidel became a word with virtually no meaning. Oh, our missionaries still use the word, and I heard it a lot when I was growing up, because Springfield, Missouri, is one of the main assembly lines for the American missionary trade, and is the headquarters of the Assemblies of God. It is also the place where John Ashcroft was born. We are the home of Baptist Bible College, Central Bible College and Evangel College. Hard working people from all over America scraped their money together and sent their children to Springfield, MO, where they were expected to take bible classes, get married and go out to spread God's word. Some of them needed to get part time jobs to help pay for their education, doing housework.

We were one of the best houses for a Baptist Bible Girl to work. Not only were my parents prominent, upstanding members of the business community, but we were Jewish. We were, to vertical religious sects obsessed with proselytizing, Trainer Infidels. The girls could practice their missionary work right here in Springfield while making minimum wage.

This is the way to picture my Barbie and me, during these years. I'm dressing my Barbie in Red Flare.

(She dresses Barbie in Red Flare. She puts her hat on her too, attaching it with a pin.)

Red Flare is a bright red coat with white satin lining, that flares. It also has a matching red hat and a clutch purse with a gold closure.

Meanwhile Denise, a sweet girl from a small town near Denver, wearing a pastel sweater and three inches below the knee wool skirt, is mopping the floor near by. God has firm and unshakable notions about a woman's knees, so there were strict dress codes at Baptist Bible College. This was not a problem. The B B C girls loved strict codes and rules, they were brought up loving them, that's how you *know*, when you're a vertical, how much you love God, by how much you love His *rules*. And when you're young, and pretty, you're just bursting to love. So. Picture Denise mopping and singing a song about Jesus just loud enough for me to make out every word, but soft enough that my mother can't hear.

The B B C girls had to be clever. My parents wouldn't allow them to try to convert their children, so they could never talk openly to us about Christ. But my *mother* was fair game. And in between the mothering they got *from* her and the cleaning they did *for* her, they proselytized *full time*. They weren't expected to actually convert her. They were expected to try. The ones who loved her—and many of them did—tried the hardest. There was one who never stopped writing her long letters begging her to accept Christ as her savior. Like clockwork those letters arrived, for thirty-five years. I was the one who had to call and let them know mom had died. I think it was an impossible thought for most of them. They had last seen her in the late 60s or 70s, in the full flush of her beauty and power. She seemed unstoppable to most everyone who met her. Mostly, she seemed blessed. We never expect the blessed to die before us. It always comes as a surprise.

When I told Denise and the others about mother, every single one of them assured me that she was in heaven. I didn't say anything. There was no heaven and my mother was not in it. But I didn't feel like explaining that to them. I wasn't in an educational mood.

My mother, on the other hand, was always in an educational mood. She never passed up a chance to tell people in Springfield what was good about Judaism, so she would have corrected Denise gently, and then used the opportunity to share with her the three improvements that a couple of thousand years ago made Judaism an important upgrade in religion, a kind of God 2.0.

TITLE:
GOD 2.0

First: There was just one God. This made worship so much more efficient, like central heating, it put the same god everywhere in your house at once, and it cut down on system conflicts.

Second: No more human sacrifice. You could no longer get to heaven by killing an unbeliever. No more ladder building using your neighbors. This is the first official step toward valuing the other as we value ourselves. I think it's the reason why everybody reacts so violently to the practice of suicide bombers, a throwback to pagan sacrifice that unsettles us down to the bottom of our souls. Even the rewards of the sacrifice—the Islamic dream of heaven—with the seventy-two virgins? That would be young girls, without experience? —gives us the creeps.

And the third great game changing upgrade on the God 2.0 program goes like this: The after life is no longer the primary focus of this one. Judaism marks the end of other worldly mindedness.

Of course, it wasn't a clean un-install. It turns out that we need our dead. This is why the lack of an operational after life was the deal breaker when it came to Judaism, even though to my way of thinking it should have been circumcision. I remember arguing with my brother about it when we were in high school. I insisted that circumcision was barbaric and aesthetically unpleasing. My brother, ignoring the reference to the pleasing part, and in any case having nothing more to lose…reminded me that it was a sacred covenant, that God gave the Jews the Torah, the great book of our people, and they in return got circumcised. I pointed out that they might have been better off going to a lending library. But without an after life with its solid hell and palpable heaven, Judaism would always have limited appeal. If we'd had a plausible exit strategy, we would probably be living in a Jewish world. But we held firm. The Jewish world is like Vegas—what happens here, stays here.

The lack of hell created many problems for the Midwestern reform Jewish child. I cannot tell you the

pity with which I was regarded by my classmates at
Eugene Field Elementary School. For I was not saved.
On a dozen different occasions, girls in my class
actually wept over this. Beverly King, who sat in front
of me for years because of alphabetical supremacy,
cried more than once. I did not believe in heaven and
consequently would not be going there. Explaining
to these decent, religious, and not stupid girls that I
didn't have to be saved because there was no afterlife
at all—well, it wasn't hard. It was impossible. What
was the point of living if you couldn't get into heaven?
What was the point of being good if being bad didn't
send you to hell? The children I grew up with lived
in a world so uncomprehendingly vertical to me—I
lived somewhere else. Our worlds looked the same
from the outside—but on the inside, where all the
real things happened, all the reasons were different. I
was sorry for them, because they believed in heaven. I
was jealous of them, because they believed in heaven.
When I asked my mother why we couldn't believe in
heaven, she said we didn't need to. We had heaven on
earth.

(She picks up Barbie.)

My mother's favorite color was red. Red was inevitable
in my mother's life because it was practically *illegal* in
my grandmother's. My grandmother dressed herself
and her home in dusky roses and pale, silken shades of
Prussian blue. My mother, who didn't know how *not*
to fall in love every day of her life, she was continually
falling in love with her husband, her children, her
house, her country—well, that kind of passion for the
world—is red. My mother didn't have a red coat, as
far as I can remember, but that is probably the only
red thing she didn't have. She had a red convertible,
several red rooms filled with red sofas, red chairs, a red
fireplace, a red kitchen—okay, it was a cross between

salmon and red, but it was almost red. Red shoes and
red handbags and red paintings, and her favorite artist
was Red Grooms. She and my father collected about
a dozen of his paintings. And now they're all about to
go on the moving van with my father to independent
living, and this house, where I grew up, is getting sold.
That's why the Barbies had to come out of the closet
where my childhood has been taking its long, long
sleep. Why I'm driving myself insane, researching the
outfits, discovering the names, like "Ski Queen", or
"Tennis, Anyone?", or "Solo in the Spotlight"—

*(She shows each of these outfits as she mentions them,
and she probably can't help playing with them a little too,
maybe even singing a bit into the microphone of Solo in the
Spotlight…)*

—sorting the accessories, matching them to the outfit,
finding out the going price, putting each outfit in a
Ziplock bag with a piece of paper with the name of the
outfit, and then—well, that's the then I don't know.

My mother held on to these, all these years. Sometimes
I think I should keep them too—but I know I can't. I
don't have the room. Tomorrow I'm going to take them
over to the guy who's fencing the rest of my childhood
on eBay. Maybe it's right that my fifty-nine vintage
Barbie outfits join the stream, the great moving river
of memory and fetish and greed that the internet has
made out of the artifacts of the American dream.

The problem with the American Dream—it's hard
waking up from it. The first part of the dream—we're
the Good Guys. We're the forces of the Enlightenment.
Slavery, eradicating the Indians, these were things that
filed down the finer points of the American soul, hell,
these were *crimes* that rubbed off Prime Soul Acreage,
it's true—we weren't perfect, we had a few things
that were *really* screwed up, but we were working on

them. And the other part of the American Dream—is
abundance. God gave us a land crammed full from
sea to shinning sea, He gave us more of every natural
resource in the world than He gave anybody—except
for one thing. A thing He apparently didn't know we'd
need so much of. Oil.

(She picks up the Dream Car.)

Here's a shocker: The Dream Car is an English car. An
Aston Martin.

(She puts Barbie into her Dream Car.)

I know, I know, but James Bond drove an Aston
Martin, and the whole double o seven thing was
huge back then. English cars, by the way, never ran
on English oil—there isn't any. So the Brits had been
drilling for oil in the Middle East since the 20s. We're
not messing around in Iraq or Iran back then because
we've got Texas and Oklahoma to keep us happy, so
we're busy drilling at home.

TITLE:
HIT AND RUN 1

Then comes World War Two. The Brits and the
Russians are in trouble. In order to save the world, we
have to get supplies to the Russians, and the only route
we can use, that isn't impassable during the winter
snows is the Persian corridor. But to get to the Persian
corridor, you need to go through Iran.

*(She pulls a Barbie sized map of Iran out of the Dream Car,
unfolds it, and indicates the Persian Corridor.)*

This means that Iran has to stay in Allied hands. So
in 1942, that's where we put it. The Shah was being
a little too friendly with Germany anyway, so we
just kick him out, politely, but kick him out we do,

we remove the ruler of a country—of course, regime
changing during war is not called regime changing,
it's called what it really is, *war*, but during war it's
okay, it's expected, so our hands are still semi-clean
on the regime changing charge. And then we turn
Iran into—like—a Wal-Mart Military super-center,
the biggest Wal-Mart in the world, we fill it up with
tanks, and guns, and jeeps, millions of tons of them, it's
supermarket sweep for the Russians, and to keep Iran
happy, we give her tons and tons of non-military stuff
like lampshades and clothing and flatware and such.
And the biggest problem we have, as the occupiers
of Iran? Traffic accidents. Traffic accidents caused by
military vehicles. Hundreds of Iranians killed by Allied
soldiers. An American diplomat explains the fatalities
like this: "The reflexes of the Iranians are relatively
slow."

TITLE:
NO COMMUNICATION WITH THE DEAD

After she died, my mother did not contact us. This
seemed unfair. Everybody I knew who'd lost someone
they loved had these stories of the way their mother or
brother or husband had contacted them from beyond
the grave. I knew that if anyone loved her family
enough to bridge the worlds, my mother did. She had
already tried to stay with us, after she'd died. When
we left the hospital, they were wheeling her body
along behind us, on their way to the hearse. Turn after
turn on the way across courtyards and hallways and
parking lots, we'd lose her, the stretcher was slower
than we were, but the attendants knew the short cuts,
and it seemed like every time we turned a corner, there
she'd be. As if we were still a family of five. And then
when we couldn't get my sister a ticket to Springfield

on the same plane as the rest of us (my mother had
died in Florida, the funeral was in Springfield), the
first seat we *could* get her turned out to be on the same
plane my mother's body was coming on. That's the
way she was. My mother didn't ever want to be alone.

When I went to the airport to pick up my sister, I
brought one of my nieces along for company. We
picked up my sister, and then I decided that we should
at least meet my Mother, even if we couldn't take
her home. I asked a scruffy looking baggage handler
where her coffin would be, and he said because of
construction detours we'd never make it to the cargo
area, but he'd go with us, to help us find the way. It
was 10:30, 11 o'clock at night, his lunch break, and
he considered briefly, before getting into the car,
calculating if he would get back in time to avoid losing
his job. He did the math, then shrugged and climbed
in. He had had a mother, once, too.

As he got in, a kind of joyriding thrill ran through the
car. I looked at my niece. She was numb with terror,
she was fourteen years old, how many times had it
been drummed into her head, never get into a car with
a stranger, and here I'd just invited one in. Of course,
the intense aliveness that slices through you after the
one who loves you best is dead makes every single
moment just vibrate with resonance. The vivid clarity
that comes after death—how the important things
assume their true size and dimension, crowding out
the unimportant things so easily—makes anything
possible. Anything except the one impossible thing you
truly want.

The baggage handler not only got us to the cargo area,
he was our Virgil, he pounded on three different doors,
went into places clearly marked NO ADMITTANCE,
he did all the lesser impossible things for us that we
never could have done. He called and got someone

to open a door for us at the *exact moment* the box
that contained my mother in her coffin came off the
transport and was carried into the cargo area. My
mother had gotten off the plane, we had put a strange
man in our car, and we had met her. We had not made
her wait. The person you're picking up at the airport
always knows how much you love them by whether
you're there on time or not. It was one of the early
miracles, one of the first things we did for our dead.

We waited with her coffin until the people from
the funeral home came. We watched as they took
her away. Then we took our guide back to the main
airport. He was forty-five minutes over his lunch
break, but he didn't care. He had taken us to see
our mother, out of love for his own. He had been
performing his own miracle for his dead.

Anyway, it gradually became clear to me that if my
mother hadn't contacted us, it was not out of an
inability to do so. Because if defying all the laws of
God and nature, if will and love were all it took to
communicate with those you left behind after death,
she would have been talking to us non-stop. We would
hardly have even known she was gone. No, it was a
choice. My mother did not *believe* in communication
with the dead, and since she always had the courage of
her convictions, she was keeping still. It shouldn't have
surprised me that she refused to contact us from the
other side. Just because she was dead was no reason to
let down her standards.

Standards are a funny thing. They are the way we have
of believing in things, out loud.

TITLE:
LAUNDRY

I have a cousin, and this cousin has no children. And so, this cousin feels that not adding to the population of the planet is a more than ample contribution to the conservation of its precious resources. Consequently, the washing machine in her house runs twelve hours a day, the house is always lit up like a Christmas tree, heat and air-conditioning blast through wide open windows spring, summer, winter and fall. When confronted about these violent squanderings of air and water and fossil fuels, my cousin merely says "I have no children who will do laundry, no grandchildren who will do laundry, no great-grandchildren who will do laundry—think of all the generations of laundry that are not going to be done because of me. So it's only fair—I get to do all the laundry I want."

And so she does. It's a part of the American Dream that we REALLY don't want to let go of—the myth that there's more where that came from. We don't want anybody telling us we can't do all the metaphoric laundry we want, no matter how much it pollutes our air and our water and our foreign policy, rampaging and pillaging like we're on Mr Toad's Wild Ride.

And we've been on that ride since World War II, a war we won with our oil as much as with American blood and guts. In battle after battle it was oil that meant victory or defeat, and as the German Panzers and U-Boats ran out of gas, the Allies surged forward on a seemingly endless river of US oil. We used so much of our oil in fact, that it put a serious dent in our reserves. So after the war we're in the Persian Gulf right alongside the English and the French, pumping out Middle Eastern oil. It's 1950. The Iranian pedestrians with the slow reflexes who were crushed

under Allied wheels are long dead and forgotten by
us, but not, of course, by the Iranians. Harry Truman
is at the wheel of America, and this is what he does to
keep us driving. He encourages a bloodless coup that
deposes the president of another nation. We're not at
war now, so this is regime changing, pure and simple.
We, the forces of freedom and democracy, help regime
change Syria, a country with no beef at all with ours,
merely because it is the only way we can get a pipeline
constructed across it. The ousted president's name?
Shukri Quwatli. A man nobody even remembers, a
man who has been all but erased from history.

And our President does one other thing to make sure
the oil will keep flowing. He promises Saudi Arabia
that if they are ever attacked by the Soviet Union, the
U S will come to their aid. This is the moment that
starts the cascade of events that will transform the
army of the greatest superpower the world has ever
known into a global oil protection service.

It is also the moment when the Saudis realize that
Standard Oil is robbing them blind. Standard Oil had
been paying the Saudis an unbelievably tiny royalty
for the oil they drilled, less than ten percent. The Saudi
reserves are the Helen of Troy of the modern world,
launching a billion ships, cars and trucks. Historians
call Standard Oil's sixty-year lease on Saudi oil
fields "the greatest material prize in human history."
Standard Oil had been allowed to exploit this treasure
unregulated for years. Now the golden goose was
about to get cooked. The Saudis say, from now on we
want fifty percent. Or no deal.

Standard Oil did not take this lying down. They went
crying went crying to Uncle Sam.

TITLE:
THE GOLDEN GIMMICK

And what did Uncle Sam do, did he make the Saudis
back down? No. Did he tell Standard Oil to grow
up and accept that the days of Astounding, Almost
Criminal Profits were over, that they were going to
have to settle for just, say, Astronomical ones from now
on? No, he didn't do that either. Our government came
up with a third party to foot the bill—the American
people. From now on, Standard Oil could deduct from
their U S taxes the amount they paid in royalties to
the Saudi government. This meant that the American
people subsidized Standard Oil, we paid them to
make a profit selling us gas, gas that was incompletely
priced, that was artificially cheap. Cheap gas may
seem like a good idea—but this was the loophole that
created our addiction to oil, destroyed our railroads,
and has driven our foreign policy for over fifty years. It
was called the Golden Gimmick. It reminds me of the
names of my Barbie outfits.

TITLE:
HERE'S WHAT I WAS DOING

Here's what I was doing in 1950, when the Golden
Gimmick first gave Standard Oil the Midas Touch:
Nothing. I wasn't born yet. Barbie wasn't either. Her
parents, whose name was Handler, wouldn't conceive
of her for several years, coincidentally around the same
time my parents conceived me. Here the similarities
between me and Barbie end.

(She takes Barbie out of the Dream Car, and undresses her.)

Barbie was modeled on the German Lilli doll, a quasi-
pornographic toy intended for adult men. This fact
is no surprise to any child who has actually played

with a Barbie, as the nasty possibilities are endless
and inevitable. The naked Barbie begs to be fondled.
The Handlers, toy manufacturers on vacation in
Germany, saw the Lillis, and thought, hmmm, maybe
American girls would like a doll that looked like a
real woman. So they brought a few Lillis home and
found a designer, named Jack Ryan. Now Jack wasn't
just any old toy designer. He was a playboy who'd
been married to Zsa Zsa Gabor, and during the Cold
War he designed the bodies of Hawk and Sparrow
missiles. Talk about the right man for the job. Work
on the Barbie—named for the Handler's daughter,
Barbara—went swiftly. There was one little snag. After
the first prototypes were designed, they were sent to
Japan to be fabricated. The Japanese factory workers
repeatedly added nipples, which caused frustration as
the American team working on the doll was forced to
file them down. Finally Jack sent a model back with the
nipples smoothed away, and the Japanese toymakers
got the hint.

Like Ken's tiny androgynous genital bulge—whose
size was completely dictated by the ergonomics of
the zippers in his pants, and not prudery, Barbie's
dimensions were similarly enforced. If Barbie were a
real person, her measurements would be 40-18-32. The
closest living human with those proportions is—

*(She asks the audience if they can imagine who this would
be. Chances are, they'll say "Dolly Parton.")*

—yes, Dolly Parton, except Dolly is a tiny little thing.
Barbie, if made to scale, would be over six feet tall.
But Barbie's bizarre, impossible body is not an insult
to all actual women—it's a necessity. When Barbie is
dressed, the elastic and cloth around her waist is just
as thick and bulky as the elastic and cloth would be on
a skirt around ours, but Barbie is one-hundredth our
size. So the huge, impossible breasts balanced on the

tiny waist stacked on top of a sliver of hips is not about body hatred or female form revulsion, even though it would later become, probably, a cause of it. It was all about the clothes. It was about the drape of the cloth, the flow of the line, the look of the design.

In 1995, Islamic fundamentalists in Kuwait issued a Fatwa against Barbie.

(She holds her hands out, as if they are scales, and lays Barbie down in one. Then she "weighs" each one.)

Barbie, Salman Rushdie. Barbie, Salman Rushdie. It's difficult to do the math.

TITLE:
UNINTENDED CONSEQUENCES

In preparation for putting my parents' house on the market, my brother comes to Springfield for the weekend to pack up the things he's taking. We're at breakfast, and I've just read, that very morning, about how we helped create the Taliban and Al Qaeda by making the Saudis give money to the C I A's clandestine campaign in Afghanistan. This meant that we, the Great Infidels, created the pipeline that funneled Saudi "charitable contributions" to militant Islamists and fathered the most violent extremist groups the world has ever known. If this were fiction, it would be called irony. In real life, of course, it's called tragedy.

Anyway, I tell my brother about this. And he just shakes his head, dismissing this demonstration of cause and effect, because we don't live in a cause and effect world, anymore, because in a cause and effect world, the person or institutions who cause the cause have to take responsibility for the effect. And nobody takes responsibility now. So my brother just shakes his head, and says the great new Get Out of Jail Free Card of the 21st century. He says, "Unintended consequences. We can't be held *responsible* for unintended consequences." And I have to stand there, with my mouth hanging open. And I have to say, as ponderously and assholically as I can: "But there's nothing *but* unintended consequences. So if we're not responsible for them, what *are* we responsible *for*?" But he's not listening to that. He doesn't have to. Nobody in America has to listen to anything they don't agree with anymore. Faith Based America and Reality Based America fought it out, Faith won, the Age of Reason vanished, and now nobody has to worry when facts and a little thing like reality contradict what they want to believe.

TITLE:
ON MY WAY TO THE CEMETERY

I am on my way to put some flowers on my mother's grave when I see a funeral procession coming from the opposite direction.

I see that it is not an ordinary funeral—there is a long line of people standing along the route, waving American flags. It is a military funeral. Someone's son has died in the war in Iraq. Someone's son will lie in the ground in the Springfield National Cemetery, which now borders the Jewish Cemetery on two sides. Someone's son has died in a land far away and will lie under the ground, a few feet from my mother. And he has died for something so big, and in the end, so small. He has died because we lack the political will to produce a widely consumable and cost effective alternative to petroleum. If we had spent the billions and billions developing an alternative, instead of policing and protecting the Middle East…

TITLE:
IMAGINE A DIFFERENT PATH

Imagine a different path. Say we hadn't treated the Middle East like our very own fossil fuel piñata. Say our government hadn't help create an entire economy dependent on artificially cheap oil. We would have developed alternative technologies. We wouldn't have destroyed our rail system, and deserted our inner cities. No car on earth would exist that got eight miles to the gallon.

Every one of our dreams, every one of our sorrows, every moment of our lives is plugged into the grid that's been betraying the America we thought we belonged to for years. The old cliché that power corrupts has a whole new meaning now. And when do we feel the most powerful?

(She picks up her Dream Car.)

When we're behind the wheel of a car.

I really would like to keep my Dream Car. I don't know how much it's worth. I can't find it listed in any of my Barbie books. Unfortunately, it's nowhere near mint. Curious that a plaything only really has value if it has never been played with. I played with it a lot, and it's many miles shy of N R F P.

(She puts Barbie in her car. She shows off the broken-off fender.)

Because at some point, we can see that Barbie has had a little fender bender. Barbie must have hit something. Something…or someone. Barbie has had a little hit and run.

TITLE:
HIT AND RUN 2

Our country did too. Our servicemen are stationed in
Iran in 1964 to pander to the Shah and keep our access
to his oil. Unfortunately, the Iranians' slow reflexes
have not gotten any quicker since 1942, and once again,
our military personnel are hitting and killing them. Of
all the insults to Iranian order and tradition, it is the
Americans' disregard for their safety that outrages the
Iranian people the most. And then America and the
Shah's government sign a SOFA, which means that U S
military personnel suspected of breaking local laws are
court-martialed by the U S military, instead of being
tried in local courts.

When the Iranian people hear that American
servicemen are now beyond the reach of Iranian law,
they go wild. A Shiite cleric named Ayatollah Ruhollah
Khomeini makes an impassioned speech. He says
that the Shah and his government have "Reduced
the Iranian people to a level lower than that of an
American dog. If someone runs over a dog belonging
to an American, he will be prosecuted. But if an
American cook runs over the Shah, the head of state,
no one will have the right to interfere with him."

The entire country rallies about Khomeini, secular
and Shiite alike, and suddenly, he is a national hero.
It takes almost no time at all for the Shah to arrest and
deport him. He flees to Paris, where he will spend his
exile honing his hatred for America to a fine, white
point. And I am at the Toy Box, on the Plaza, carefully,
tenderly taking Enchanted Evening off the shelf like it's
the Holy Grail, blissful, and oblivious, my life nested
like a pearl, dead center in the magic oyster bed of the
baby boom.

TITLE:
WHY I HAVE SO MANY BARBIE OUTFITS

(She surveys all her Barbie outfits.)

Some of you may be wondering why I have so many
Barbie outfits. Why on earth any child would need so
many.

Well, it's because of my older sister. She refused to
let my mother buy her a Barbie doll. She was a pre-
teen proto-feminist who didn't have time to play with
Barbie—she was going to be the first female supreme
court justice. She had homework to do. My brother
was going to be the first Jewish president. He did his
homework too. I was going to be. Period. Just be. Be
here now was also an alternative life goal. Along with
being with the one I loved, and if that didn't work out,
loving the one I was with. I had no idea what any of
those songs really meant, but they meant everything.
I was having far too much fun imagining what they
meant to do homework. But it turned out I was just
saving up for the homework I've been doing now,
for the months and days of research that a person
does when their country goes to war, and they have
to figure out why somebody far away hates them so
much, and why they didn't see it coming in time. It's
a homework assignment because it's about home,
because your country is your home.

My mother really thought that. She had a kind of
mythic boundary loss, she didn't know where our
family stopped, and where America began. She
worked in the family business full time, and always
ran an arts organizations or a charity or two. But she
was never too busy to take me to the Toy Box—she
had been denied the opportunity to buy Barbies for
my sister so she bought me my share of them, and my
sister's too. The occasional sightings, of me, dressing

up my dolls, making up stories—that made her happy, I think. I think for her it was the natural progression of the American dream: A chicken in every pot. Two cars in every garage. Five Barbies in every little girl's arms.

TITLE:
OIL MADE AMERICA WHAT SHE IS TODAY

But every part of that dream is now dependent on oil. Imagine an America built without cheap, abundant oil, and you are no longer imagining America. No malls, no suburbs, no Home Depots. Oil is more than the engine that runs our economy. It *is* our economy. No oil, no America. Unless you're living naked in a hut in a glade somewhere, your life, and the oil flow, are enmeshed. You're married, baby. You're in bed with oil, and waving a sign saying "Not in our Name" protesting the war means you're an idiot. The next time you start to get all enraged about the fact that our government is in Big Oil's pocket, the next time you feel outrage over their latest environmental disaster, the next time you demand justice in your name, just remember: it's all being done in your name already. It's in your name the second you take a pill, use a computer, or get dressed. It's in your name when you buy a toy for your child or put her cheerios in a Ziplock bag. Not in My Name? That's a fairy tale we're way too old to believe in.

Peak production of oil will occur in as early as five years or as late as 2030. Some experts believe it is peaking right now. That means that half of all the oil on earth is already gone. That's why every country that is addicted to oil, and China is now pushing ahead of us to the front of that line, every petrochemically addicted country will soon start acting the way addicts act when the supply runs out—committing unspeakable crimes to get hold of what's left.

It's a shame petrochemicals aren't more like gold, isn't it? In the old days, it was standard practice to just melt your old idols down and make new ones when a new God came to town. You can recycle plastic, but you can't turn it back into oil. Think of the billions of Barbies out there—billions and billions of them. We could run the country for a year, if we could just get the oil back by melting a billion little household goddesses down.

(She picks up Barbie's Dream house.)

TITLE:
ONCE I LIVED IN BARBIE'S HOUSE

I lived in Barbie's house once. I lived there for several months. I don't mean in my mind, in my fantasy. I mean in Barbara Handler's actual house—her parents bought it for her in the 70's after her messy divorce.

(She unfolds the Dream House and sets it up.)

It was a small two-story cottage in a gorgeous New England town next door to an artists colony, and when I lived there the colony had just bought it, and was in the process of colonizing it. Barbara lived there for ten unhappy years. Alcohol was involved in this unhappiness, and often. Guns also played their part. During the colony's early years we never tired of doing the Barbie Bullet Above the Refrigerator re-enactment. The story we told went like this: He came home drunk. Barbie was waiting for him, drunker.

I imagine she was wearing, when she got home from the bar that night, a western cowgirl outfit—tight jeans, red high-heeled hand tooled cowboy boots, and a fringed suede jacket. I don't have this Barbie outfit, by the way. I wish I did. Fringe was the first clothes drying system, evolved by Native Americans as a brilliant method for wicking moisture away from the body of the garment, to dry the shirt out. There was no drying Barbie out, however.

(She dresses Barbie in Nighty Negligee.)

She changed into Nighty Negligee, stock number 965, manufactured in 1962, as soon as she got home, hoping that her current Ken would walk in the door and the clouds of pink chiffon would encircle them in a floating sea of pastel love. He didn't, so she kept drinking. She hugged her little stuffed dog—

(She holds up the dog.)

—an adorable pink pup with blue ears and a black pearl nose—close to her cool, perfect breasts which are just barely visible beneath the teasing peek-a-boo pink folds, and she drinks some more.

Hours later, half passed out on her empty bed, she hears his car pull up in the drive.

(She grabs a Ken doll, and brings him over to the Dream House.)

The rage wells up inside her. She grabs a gun from the bedside table. Still clutching her little pink dog, she staggers to the top of the stairs. Ken crashes in through the back door. She floats—or so it would seem to someone watching her in her billowing, sleep wrinkled sad chiffon—she floats down the stairs and aims. She fires. The shot goes wild, it lodges above the refrigerator, where the bullet will remain, a source of entertainment for colonists in years to come. She fires again. This time her aim is true, and it lodges in his knee. He goes down. He screams. She screams. No one hears the shots or the screaming because there's no one living next door, the artists colony isn't there yet, it's 1979.

It's 1979, and in Iran the U S embassy is under siege. Frantic diplomats are making frantic calls. The embassy is taken over. Islamic militants burn the American flag in front, while hostages are herded from room to room inside.

Barbie drops the gun, calls 9-1-1, and crumples in a puddle of pink on the floor to await the police.

She does not look so good in her mug shot. Barbie is pushing forty, and life has not been all that kind to her. Her face shows the drink and the disappointment and the years.

A china doll, barring an accident, holds its looks. Put it on a shelf, it will look the same forty years later as it did when you put it there. Not a Barbie. Maybe the plastic we make now will last for centuries, but we were just learning how to use petrochemicals when we started making things like Barbie dolls, and a lot of the soft plastics we made then degrade. Barbie's body is still great—made of a slightly different, harder kind of plastic. It's the face that shows the ravages of time. The lipstick is smeary and looks clumsily applied. The eye makeup is eroding, the bright blue eye shadow running into the smudged eyeliner. The forty year-old Barbie doll, with rare exceptions, looks exactly the way the forty year-old drunken, lipstick smeared Barbara looked that night.

I usually watch T V while I sort my Barbie outfits. We have two huge T Vs, one in the family room—which has a red fireplace and red furniture, and one in the red room, which has…I'll leave that to your imagination. It's hard to understand that the house will be sold, that another family will live here. My parents built it, and every time she drove up the street, my mother would look at it, and say, as if it were a brand new thought, as if she were discovering it for the first time: "It's a nice house." Every single time. Lately, whenever I drive up the street, just before I turn into the driveway, I hear her say it, so I say it with her. It's a nice house.

TITLE:
THE HOUSE OF SAUD IS FALLING DOWN

I've matched as many Barbie shoes as is humanly possible, and still have about a dozen pairs left. The shoes were always the problem with Barbie. They always fell off and the dog was getting them or your mother was sucking them up in the vacuum cleaner. If you played with other girls, you could never keep track of whose shoes were whose. It's a Sunday, so while I randomly put shoes into bags with outfits they couldn't possibly go with, I watch Face the Nation. They're talking about the monarchy in Saudi Arabia, the trouble it's in. One of the guests says that the House of Saud has already begun to fall. Soon there will be a coup, the royal family will be out, and Saudi Arabia will not be called Saudi Arabia anymore.

And then it hits me. Saudi Arabia is called Saudi the way George Forman's Grill is called George Forman's. Because it belongs to the Saudi Family.

It is one of the great ironies of the war in Iraq that we really didn't go to war to have access to Iraq's oil fields. We went to retain our access to Saudi Arabia's. Saddam Hussein in power threatened Saudi Arabia's monarchy, and made our relations with the house of Saud and its oil precarious. So—Hussein had to go. The research makes it clear—the plans for regime change in Iraq were in the works long before 9/11.

TITLE:
WE HAVE TO BELIEVE THAT IT'S OIL

Of course, the thing about research is—when you're searching for a clear, unobstructed way to understand something, you tend to find it. And you just ignore the facts that clutter up the view. But the research I did made it clear: The point is not that we're dependent on oil, the point is that the price we've paid for this dependency turns out to be some of the finest parts of the American soul, we've sold ourselves down a river of oil. But we can save ourselves. We can save the world. All we lack is the political will. All we lack is the courage to jump off the run-away stagecoach before it goes over the cliff. You've seen that movie since you were a kid. You know what happens if you don't jump in time.

We have to believe that it's oil. Because if we don't, we won't change. We won't sacrifice. We won't jump in time. I know it's sloppy thinking to say that everything that's wrong with America will suddenly be okay if we change the way we think about oil. But sometimes you're falling and you need somebody to throw you something. You need a rope. A rope's not very wide. But it's easier to throw than, say, an entire marble staircase. Oil is the only rope I know of that can get the job done.

You know all that deck furniture we've been rearranging on the Titanic? You know what I'm talking about. Your 401K's, your children's college funds, your hours at the gym, your non-surgical facelift? You really think any of that's going to make a difference when the Saudi oil stops flowing?

And I have no right to preach to anyone about any of this.

I have an S U V.

A few years ago I was driving to the store for a gallon of milk and got hit by a teenager, and some deck furniture impulse made me go out and buy something big, something huge, something that I thought would be unsinkable, in a car crash sort of way. Never mind that S U V's aren't safer for the occupants, just more dangerous for those in the cars they hit, I *felt* safer. It isn't even a big S U V, as S U Vs go—it's a Pathfinder. And I love that Pathfinder.

But. The Pathfinder has to go. I'm putting an ad in the newspaper. I'm letting it go.

Let me say again. I love my Pathfinder. I really, really do. I spend a lot of time, moving from place to place in it. I'm like a lot of people, who spend more time in their cars than they do in bed. I think most people spend more time in their cars than they do in love.

I don't take the Pathfinder when I go to the cemetery.

I use my dad's car sometimes, but usually I ride my bike or walk. The cemetery is so close to our house, it's almost impossible to go anywhere without passing it. I know I go there too often. I know it's time to move on. I move on in my own way. I move on from spring flowers like peonies and phlox to summer flowers like lilies and lisianthus to fall flowers like cosmos and mums.

(She takes out a few photos of flowers at her mother's grave, and looks at them.)

Each time, a small miracle. It's an ancient ritual, who knows how long we've been doing it, bringing flowers to our dead. Who knows when one day it will work. When the small miracles build up, a hundred billion, a billion billion small, every day miracles. Someday, not for me, but for somebody, the miracle will work.

My brother comes down to Springfield again. We
divide up the linens, the silver, the crystal. I say to him,
"Do you know what we're doing in the Middle East,
do you know we've been regime changing for years?"
I give him the facts and the dates, the incredible things
we've done, in the name of oil, for over fifty years, and
I expect him to register, if not shock, at least righteous
indignation.

But he doesn't. Instead, he just says, patiently, as if I'd
asked him why night follows day, "We needed the oil,
Sherry. We had to protect our access to it." This scares
me. I say, "but the oil's not *ours*." This scares *him*. He
looks at me like *I'm* crazy. I look at him like *he's* crazy.
And then I go get him some more bubble wrap for the
sterling silver punch bowl.

Sometimes, when I get really scared, I calm myself
down by thinking about Greed. I think we can count
on it. Greed is what got us into this mess, and Greed
is what can get us out of it. I have hopes that some
really smart, *really* greedy people are right now
cooking up a way to make a fortune in the new "post-
petroleum economy." If they hurry, they might even
be able to come up with an alternative to oil before
global warming or a giant oil eco disaster kills us all.
Yes, I think we can count on Greed. But that's just an
indication of how scared I am.

TITLE:
I'VE BEEN SCARED FOR A LONG TIME

I've been scared for a long time. I've been scared since
the Israeli Olympic team was slaughtered when I was
in High School. Since that day, I have never found
myself in a room with more than ten Jews without
checking for alternative exits, calculating the height of

the windows, and identifying objects that could serve
as possible weapons in a crisis. Imagine how hard it is
to shop at Zabars under these conditions. When I walk
into a temple or synagogue, I still do a quick calculus
on the bullet deflecting density of prayer books and
pew backs. I keep an eye out for old, frail people and
children to fling out of harm's way.

1979. There's a revolution in Iran. The Shah is
overthrown, which means the Ayatollah Khomeini,
who has been in exile since 1964 when he spoke
out against the Status of Forces Agreement, returns
triumphantly to Tehran and wastes no time whipping
up resentment against the U S. Then President Carter
makes an incredible political blunder. He responds
with compassion to the Shah's request to come to
America for treatment of his advanced cancer. Anti-
Americanism spikes as rumors spread that the Shah's
illness is just a sham, dreamed up to mask a C I A plot
to return the Shah to power.

The U S embassy in Tehran is seized by Islamist
militants. They take fifty-two hostages. Frantic
embassy employees, shredding madly up until the
last second, manage to destroy the most sensitive
documents, just before they're overrun.

*(She might take some of the shredded packing materials she
has in a box, and, in all the chaos of the attack, dump them
out, making a little pile of shredded paper.)*

No one dreamed the occupation, a symbolic gesture,
would last more than a week. But Khomeini hates
the U S, and he publicly endorses the seizure of the
embassy. And then one of the occupying militants,
who has been staring at the piles of shredded
documents, gets a brilliant idea. Expert carpet weavers
are brought in, women who magically weave the
shredded paper back into documents. Documents

which seem to imply that the U S *is* plotting the Shah's return. The hostage crisis goes from weeks to months, months to over a year.

In a move that demonstrated an unerring sense of bad timing, I was living in L A in 1979, and when Iran stopped exporting oil, the gas shortage hit L A, home of the freeway, especially hard. I had a small car, a Toyota Corolla, it got pretty good mileage and was easy to push when I ended up in a long line that snaked for blocks around a gas station. Jimmy Carter put on a sweater and turned down the thermostat in the White House. On T V and in the press, there was all this talk about solar cells and wind power and electric cars—if oil made our enemies strong and us weak, we would stop using it, it was as simple as that. No one was going to hold America over a barrel, especially a barrel of oil.

I had a friend named Jeff who owned a luxury condo on the beach, and we used to get high, and take ice sculptures—he always kept three or four in his freezer, a mermaid, a clamshell, a giant lobster—and go down to the Jacuzzi, turn on the jets and watch the sculptures bob and disintegrate. Jeff could afford the luxury condo and the ice sculptures because he worked for Rand, the government think tank in Santa Monica. He was a super brain, an M I T boy, he was paid a huge salary because he was on the hottest team Rand had, working on something of vital importance to the U S government: how we would continue to get an uninterrupted supply of oil when World War III broke out in the Middle East. Not if. When.

It is difficult to be scared when you are thoroughly baked, watching a mermaid bob in a Jacuzzi. But I managed. And I wasn't alone. In homes all across the country, Americans were starting to get scared. They were starting to ask, "How did it come to this?" And "Why didn't we see it coming?"

And they were starting to ask something else, too: "Why do they hate us so much?" But when Khomeini took control of our Embassy, he was only picking up where he had left off in 1964. America was his enemy. This was obvious. Except over here. Suddenly, it seemed to Americans, we were hated. *Suddenly*, as if from nowhere.

Think of that hate like a string of pearls. Think of America, putting one after the other in place. Start with 1943, go to 1950, then to the Status of Forces Agreement that enrages and creates the power of Khomeini in 1964.

String your way here from that.

TITLE:
ONE OF THE LAST THINGS

One of the last things we do for our dead is pick out the clothes their body will wear in the casket. I picked out a blue two-piece dress for my mother—it wasn't super dressy, but it was nice enough. If it were a Barbie outfit, it would have had a name like—Lunch with Midge at the Olive Garden. It had a little pattern on it, white anchors. Mom wore it a lot. She felt comfortable in it. She had prettier things, but I picked it for that.

I also picked out—a bra. Underwear. A slip. Hose—but they told me, no shoes. No need for shoes. The coffin is closed from the waist down. Wherever the dead are going, they will not be walking there. And—a pair of earrings. Jewelry is chief among a woman's treasures. And to bury your mother with treasure seems right. I stood there, for a long time, in front of her jewelry box. I tried to pick what I thought she would want.

It's hard, to understand, at that moment, in particular,
when you are touching the things that your mother
wore next to her body, it's hard to understand that
it doesn't really matter, anymore, to her. It's hard to
understand that these things no longer matter to the
dead. You go through your mother's closet, through
the dresser, the shelves, her jewelry box. It is a small
stack, a very small pile of things, you hold it in your
hands and you feel how small. Then you hand it to the
people at the funeral parlor. It's hard because there is
no miracle about it at all. It feels less like a miracle than
just about anything you know.

If I were picking out clothes for Barbie to be buried in,
I'd put her in this.

(She takes out Senior Prom.)

This was my favorite Barbie outfit. It came in another
color, but it seems I passed up the rare, practically
priceless apricot and marigold version, and instead
bought the common, easy to find emerald green and
sapphire blue one. Its name is Senior Prom.

(She dresses Barbie in Senior Prom.)

I wouldn't be going to my Senior Prom. I would be
asked, of course, Greg, the boy next door, asked me,
but it was a standing rule in our house—no dating
non-Jews. And there weren't any Jews at Glendale
High School, except my brother, my sister, and me.
Greg took somebody else.

After mother died there was a package from Greg,
he lives in Minnesota now. In it were four envelopes,
he didn't know all our different addresses, so he sent
them all together to Daddy. He'd sent each one of us
a letter: my father, my sister, my brother. Me. A man
I had not exchanged a word with in over thirty years
wrote me about my mother. About the way she looked,
handing a plate of cookies over the backyard fence. I

think that in the end, it's the kindnesses you remember the longest, about a person. About a moment. About a dress. About a funeral. About an unlived prom.

(She puts Barbie into the Dream Car.)

TITLE:
WHEN SOMETHING WONDERFUL ENDS

It was a bitter spring day when we buried my mother. It could have been warm and beautiful, but it was not.

The three of us children each spoke about my mother. I told a story about Henry James. Someone asked him for advice, about how to live in the world. He said, "You only have to know three things. One. You must always be kind. Two. You must always be kind. Three. You must always be kind."

Our mother's kindness was the earth on which we stood. We never doubted its power or its constancy, it was unconditional, like her love. She never doubted for an instant that goodness had the power to change the world.

When something wonderful ends, you look desperately for the thing you could have done to stop it. My mother died, in an instant, from something so small. From a hole the size of a pinprick, they say it was probably a congenital weakness, always there, waiting, in her brain. That there was nothing we could have done. It's hard to understand that a life can drain out, so quickly. That the life of someone you love can slip away as fast, and as impossible to stop as the flickering lives of the images of people dying on T V vanish, in a war, far away.

When something wonderful ends, we need to know why it happened. If we know why it happened, there's a chance we can do something about taking better care of all the something wonderfuls we still have left.

Let's grow up. Let's put the toys, all the toys, away.

(She packs up all the Barbie clothes that are left and starts putting them away. She closes up the Dream House.)

Let's re-claim our lost soul acreage. Our government has failed us, is failing us, and will continue to fail us. Until we make it clear we're willing to change, to sacrifice. The thing about change is, it hurts. It hurts every day. It doesn't get necessarily better. That's not something we're used to. We're used to the Dream Life lived in the Dream Car. In the day, we're resplendent in Red Flare. In the evening, we knock 'em dead in Enchanted Evening. At night, we slip into Nighty Negligee, and if our Dream Date doesn't show up, on *our* terms, the way *we* want him—we take out our guns and start shooting. It's time we got it through our heads—there are no more dream dates where energy is concerned, and we are never again getting into a car that uses petrochemicals without understanding that it is a gun, and it is pointed at our heads.

Change is a kind of miracle. You have to believe in it first, before it can exist. In order for it to happen, you have to act like it already has. That's where the vertical nations have the edge on us. They aren't afraid of paying for the things they've decided are good. They know about the unseen, and how to act like it's the realest thing in the room.

They know how to believe in miracles.

My mother did too. She knew about the miracle of everyday life, of knowing what matters and what does not. Her only regret in life was that she was not much of a writer. She talked all the time about writing her autobiography, though. She already had the title. My mother could not bear to leave us, but we had all grown up and moved away from Springfield. Everybody assumed she would outlive my father, and that when she died, and was buried next to him, there would be no one here left after her. The title of her autobiography was: "No One To Tend My Grave."

I have tried to tend it. With both hands, and a full heart, while the world ends, I have tried to tend her grave. I have tried to make a miracle. Just a small one, I admit that. But that's the point of the ritual, after all. It's why we need our dead, what we use them for.

(She puts the Dream Car, with Barbie in it, into a a large box. It's a rectangular box that's longer than it is tall, with a lid that closes the way a hinged lid closes. She closes the box. All the Barbie toys are packed away.)

It's time we grew up, and learned to tend our graves. Our dead, the 9/11 dead, the Iraqi and Afghanistan war dead, both sides. Let us claim them all for ours. And honor them, as it is our right and obligation to do.

Let us honor them by making a miracle. Let the miracle we do for our dead be that we save the world.

(Something happens to the light. Maybe it's golden and magical. Maybe it's something else. Then, dozens of pictures of the flowers on her mother's grave, perhaps in a progression: spring, summer, fall or perhaps in no order at all, ripple across the stage.)

(Fade to blackout)

END OF PLAY

www.ingramcontent.com/pod-product-compliance
Lightning Source LLC
Chambersburg PA
CBHW070033110426
42741CB00035B/2749